Psychic Development

Psychic Development for Beginners, How to Awaken your Third Eye, and Unlock and Develop your Psychic Abilities!

Table of Contents

Introduction

Thank you for taking the time to pick up this book on psychic development!

This book covers the topic of psychic development, and will teach you how to begin improving and developing your own psychic abilities!

Psychic abilities exist in all of us to varying degrees. The vast majority of people however, push these abilities to the side, and ignore them. Over time, their skills deteriorate and they become detached from the abilities they once possessed.

It is possible though, to re-train yourself to not only experience these abilities again, but to further develop them.

This book aims to educate you not only on the many different psychic abilities that exist, but also to assist you in developing them yourself. You will be provided with a range of different methods for further developing yourself and your abilities, and in no time will be very in-tune with the universe and the different things it is trying to communicate to you.

Once again, thanks for taking the time to read this book, I hope you find it to be helpful, and I wish you the best of luck on your journey.

Chapter 1:
Who can be Psychic?

Psychic energy and power is knowing or feeling something, although you don't have a logical reason to. This can be a frequency or vibration that you sense, a quiet voice speaking to you in your mind, or even a picture that pops into your head. This can come through many different senses, such as sound, sight, or touch. This is a useful skill to have, and we should always pay attention to these insights. We will talk more about why this is important later, but essentially doing so aligns you with your deeper self, helping you solve issues in your life and also blossom as a person.

Releasing Doubt and Negativity through these Skills:

Honing these skills can help you release and reduce negative forces around you, along with aiding you in accessing your imagination and true creativity. It can also:

- **Help you remove barriers:** We all construct barriers in our minds using logic and over thinking. These are useful at times, but can also get in the way of our intuition and ability to see the larger picture. Getting back in touch with your psychic abilities and intuition can help you break down these counterproductive walls.

- **Heal yourself:** Oftentimes, we undergo emotional or physical distress, without knowing how to solve it or what to do to heal the issue. When you develop these extra senses, you will receive answers for exactly how to heal your woes (and at times, the woes of others). For many of us with physical ailments, they have an emotional or mental root. Accessing our subconscious minds through psychic practices can help us find the answers we need to heal these problems and experience a fuller state of health.

- **Empower you:** Every person in this world, and every event within it, is connected through universal energy. This includes all of your actions and thoughts, which are constantly affecting more than just you. Once you realize this, that information can empower you, it will help you to make the right choices, and take actions that comes from a place of wisdom. You will no longer have to live your life feeling separate and alienated from the world, but will, instead, sense the reality that you are a part of it, and that it's a part of you.

This chapter will be about intuitive and psychic development, which often go hand in hand, and may be considered by some to be the same thing. When we hear the word "psychic", we often think that it's a special concept that only a select few people can access, but we are going to challenge that notion. The fact is that these abilities are not reserved only for a select few, but are available to each and every person in this world.

Everyone can Access their Psychic Abilities:

An example of a psychic ability is the power to heal on a spiritual level, and contrary to what you or others may think, all humans share this gift. Thinking of these abilities as gifts that only certain people can access only keeps them out of our reach. These talents are lying dormant in every single one of us, and it's only a matter of learning how to access, recognize, and develop them.

<u>**Different Ways this Happens (or Doesn't):**</u>

- **Spiritual Practice:** Some may find developing psychic abilities and intuitive powers happens through using mantras, yogic breathing, or other spiritual exercises, while others might find that prayer is the most effective method. We will explore some specific ways that you can start to access your birthright; psychic abilities.

- **Psychic Abilities as a Goal or Side Effect:** Some methods are oriented specifically toward growing psychic abilities, and others may have a different focus, yet still end up leading to intuitive powers and psychic phenomena. If you, for example, practice breathing deeply and intensely for a long time, with no objective but enlightenment, you may still develop psychic abilities.

- **Interest or Lack of Interest:** Although every person can learn how to develop this within themselves, not everyone is particularly interested in doing so, or their destiny may not have it in store for them. It might be of more importance that someone of this nature first experience and develop a certain skill that does not relate to psychic material directly, but perhaps has an indirect relationship to psychic skills. All activities can generally be improved in one way or another with the assistance of psychic development.

Are Psychic Skills always a Good thing?

The truth is that psychic skills are not inherently a good or bad thing. It's all about the way people use them that determines whether they will be something positive or negative. For example, if one uses a psychic skill to glimpse a patient's aura before healing them spiritually, using their special sight to figure out which area needs healing, it's obviously a positive use of the skill. However, these skills can also be used in selfish or vindictive ways, such as satisfying greed or hurting another on purpose, which are obviously negative ways to use that power. Like any other skill, it's all in how it's used that determines whether it's a positive or negative force.

Enlightenment and How it Relates to Psychic Phenomena:

Although not everyone would consider these concepts related, they are inextricably entwined, and it's actually impossible to become enlightened without developing your psychic skills first.

- **Setting Aside Psychic Skills:** In order to reach enlightenment, these psychic skills must be set aside, excluding those that can help others. Only this will bring true and real enlightenment to the seeker, the ultimate goal of a yogi. This stage of experiencing psychic phenomena cannot and should not be bypassed.

- **Many Paths Exist:** Most enlightenment seekers know that countless paths exist to reaching enlightenment, and that there is no single path that can give the whole truth. Each way contains its own version of the truth. Many paths may offer psychic powers such as clairaudience or clairvoyance, but according to the ultimate path of enlightenment, these are not to be seen as the end goal.

Seeking psychic skills as the end goal may be suitable for some, but for those seeking the path of true enlightenment, they should only be used in specific scenarios. This is something that only you can figure out for yourself, and should know intimately before you proceed to develop these skills.

How does Intuition differ from Development of Psychic Skills?

Similar to nearly all words, the concept of intuition is thought of in different ways by different individuals.

- **Where does Intuition come from?** You can see it as the divine speaking to you, using your consciousness, or your higher self communicating with you. Some see these things as one and the same manifestation. Psychic skills rely heavily on intuition, and learning how to hear and listen to it.

- **A Spiritual Gift:** Intuition is a spiritual gift that all humans have, but psychic skills do not necessary have to be spiritual at all. Looking at it this way, our intuition is precious and invaluable, perhaps our best skill as human beings. This is because we can recognize the true nature of reality using this way of seeing.

Intuition, more than anything else, allows you to discern truth or falsity in any given situation. The hardest part of this is actually hearing that still inner voice, behind the chaos and distraction surrounding us each day of our lives. Once we hear that voice, we must then learn how to recognize what we are hearing and respect it. It is too common for people to mistake that which they wish to hear for the true voice of intuition. This may lead to actions which are not aligned with your higher self, but instead are selfish in nature.

Developing Intuition - an Important part of Psychic Skill:

Since developing intuition is necessary for learning how to develop psychic skills, the first step is figuring out how to use it. It isn't a matter of gaining something you don't already have, but tapping into something that has always been there and always will be. Later on in this book, we will get to other methods for developing psychic skill, but this is the most important step of all.

- **You are Smarter than you Think:** Intuition is a matter of realizing that you are smarter than you give yourself credit for. Think about your body and all its physical functions. You don't have to think or strive to make your heart pump blood, or your lungs function; these processes happen on their own. Think of your intuition as another automatic skill gifted to you by life itself.

- **Remember to Listen:** The most crucial step here is to remember to listen to your intuition. It is the quiet voice that speaks to you in the midst of chaos, or the slight gut feeling you have that something isn't right. If you aren't used to listening to this, it might be hard to pick out at first. However, the more you tune into this voice, the louder it will seem, and the easier it will be to discern.

- **Act on What you Hear:** Of course, hearing wisdom is useless unless it is supported with action. The more often you actually take action based on your intuition, the stronger this force will become, and the easier it will be to figure out the right steps in any situation. When you give your intuition enough credit to listen to what it says, and then take action upon it, you give your intuitive capabilities a chance to grow and bloom.

- **The Importance of Truth:** Listening to your intuition, and taking the time to hone this skill, is at its core a pursuit of truth. Learning to be truthful and dedicating yourself to that path, above all else, will draw more of the same to you. When you accept nothing but the truth, you will further attract it, and recognize it instantly.

- **Make sure your Motives are Pure:** Having honest intentions and motives is necessary for learning how to recognize and use your skills of intuition. If you truly wish to access spiritual reality, and want to use that skill to help people, and put in plenty of effort and practice, you will find it.

Once you have gotten better at seeing, recognizing, and acting on your intuitive callings, you are already well on your way to becoming psychic. Being psychic essentially means that you see that which is beyond the surface, and most of this relies on listening to what is going on inside of you.

Chapter 2:
Signs you May already have Psychic Abilities

Have you ever had the feeling that you already have some psychic skills or abilities? Perhaps you have plenty of experiences with déjà vu that you don't believe are significant, or you think that each time you accurately predict something, it's a mere coincidence. Are you guilty of ignoring unusual events that happen to you, or do you actually pause to look deeply? Many of us who already have psychic skills in one way or another do not recognize them for what they are, and so they go unused or worse, unnoticed. Recognizing the skills that you may already have is crucial for this path.

<u>Why do People Ignore their Psychic Abilities?</u>

- **Afraid to be seen as "Weird":** Our world does not always glorify or praise higher seeing, which may lead some people to hold back their abilities out of fear of being seen as different or weird. People do not always appreciate it when others see more than they do, and may resent someone who sees deeply into reality and is open about it. When you don't have friends around who understand this interest of yours, it can be hard to listen to your intuition or stay faithful to your path.

- **Psychics are, at Times, seen as "Evil":** At times, people with psychic abilities are even seen as witches, evil, or interested in the black arts, which is not necessarily true at all. As mentioned earlier, everyone has these abilities, but most aren't aware of how to see them for what they are, haven't noticed them, or simply ignore them on purpose. However, some people may call these abilities evil, which will lead some to hide their skills. It's important to remember that these skills are not evil at all and are just a natural part of being a human.

It's also possible that the person with psychic abilities may be called crazy or nonsensical if they are open about their skills or use them in front of others. It's a shame that we live in a world that downplays such an important and natural gift, but being aware of some of the stigma against these abilities can help you move past being held back by it. Once you develop along your psychic path, these judgments from others will not matter to you as much.

<u>Signs that you have Psychic Skills:</u>

For someone who naturally has these abilities in a large amount, they can only be held back for so long before they come out. Read over some of these signs and symptoms that might mean you already have some of these abilities. Perhaps you will realize that you're already halfway there, and only need to know what you should be looking for. Once you are aware of what these skills look like, you can move onto developing them even further, or choosing which you want to focus on. Do any of these descriptions fit you?

- **Higher than Average Intuitive Abilities:** Have you heard the phone ring and already knew who it was, before seeing their name on the caller ID? Perhaps you can sense it when a text message is about to be sent to you, or have known an event was coming before anyone else. If you have the ability to sense whether someone has good or bad energy from across the room, before even speaking with them, you have highly developed intuition. This is, as mentioned earlier, the first step on the journey of uncovering all of your psychic abilities.

- **Visions Occur Regularly to you:** For someone with psychic abilities, visions can be quite normal and occur often. If you've envisioned the future on multiple occasions, whether in dreams or waking life, you definitely have some level of psychic skill. These visions may depict what is happening in the next hour, or the next few months, and are significant at times, and seemingly trivial at others. In order to test this, start noting down your visions and ideas of what is going to happen, to see if you can confirm them later on.

- **Déjà vu is Normal to you:** Déjà vu is something that everyone has experienced at least once, but for someone with higher than average psychic abilities, it's a common occurrence. If you always feel as though you've seen this place before when you really haven't, or sense familiarity in new things, places, or people, you are probably going through déjà vu. This is a signal that your psychic abilities are already in tune. Once your psychic abilities are heightened even more, this might become an everyday occurrence for you.

- **Accurate Gut Feelings on a Regular Basis:** For someone with psychic abilities, knowing what will happen before it does, is natural. You may be able to tell how events will play out, even if it's just a general sense of "good" or "bad". You may even be able to sense when you are going to get along well or badly with someone just from looking at them, or in extreme cases, sense when a natural disaster is about to hit across the world.

- **Occurrences of Telepathy:** Have you ever felt as though your mind can send messages to other people? Have you picked up the thoughts or emotions of others seemingly without any effort? Perhaps you have noticed that you are having a connection with someone else without even saying one word, or have engaged in a full conversation with someone without talking at all. These are all signs of being psychic, and skills that can be strengthened with effort and practice.

- **Vivid Dreaming:** When someone has psychic skills, they often also have a tendency to experience vivid dreams, which they can recall even after waking up, in detail. They see symbols in these vivid dreams that can show deep metaphorical significance to the dreamer, and also show hidden messages that pertain to what is happening in their life at the time. A lot of people even have dreams that recur and tell a story that is hidden within the subconscious mind. Tapping into this skill can lend valuable insights to your own mind.

- **Sensing History of Objects or People:** Being able to sense the history of an object or person after touching it or them is another psychic skill that you may naturally possess. One way in which psychics are so powerful is because they are able to sense facts about objects, places, or people by simply focusing. They sometimes are able to hug someone or hold their hand and suddenly experience or sense pieces of that person's past.

- **Premonitions and Predictions:** If you've ever recorded thoughts down because you knew they were going to occur later on, and then seen them happen, this is quite obviously proof of a latent psychic ability.

You could have known they were coming from a dream you had, or simply a feeling that appeared to come out of nowhere.

- **You know when Trouble is Coming:** There is a strong feeling that happens when someone senses their loved one in danger. This can cause you to panic for no apparent or immediate reason, and cause a huge impact on you. There might be no instant explanation for this feeling, other than the overwhelming sense that someone close to you is in trouble. In some cases, you might know who it is specifically, while for others, you will simply know it's someone close to you.

- **You feel Events from Far Away:** This ability is quite advanced and tells you that you are definitely psychic. Perhaps once you were either at work or at home, and could sense something happening from far away, either in another city or even country. If you've felt experiences from across the globe and knew what was going on, right as it happened, you likely have very advanced psychic skills. This could have been anything from a detailed, clear vision, to a strong sense of trouble happening somewhere specific.

- **You have Healing Abilities:** Some psychic people are able to touch someone ill or suffering and notice that they feel better almost instantly. Someone with psychic gifts has strong and usually positive energy that can be used to heal either mental or physical wounds in other people. If this has happened to you, it's likely the cause of your psychic abilities.

- **You Predict Future Events:** This one is quite obvious, but being able to predict future events, telling them to someone close to you, then seeing the event actually occur, is one main way to tell that you have psychic abilities. These intuitions often come at the most unexpected of times, and often without rhyme or reason, until the event occurs and makes it clear for you.

- **Having Access to Sounds:** Hearing sounds when no one else can, and always wondering why nobody is reacting to those subtle chimes or rings, can tell you that you have latent psychic skills. These noises might be pointing to an event that is yet to come. Some people with this skill are been able to narrow down what each sound means and use it to their advantage, or to help other people.

Possessing psychic abilities need not make you afraid or anxious. These skills are wonderful gifts and, when developed fully, can be used in extraordinary ways. Psychic people are very helpful and valuable to others that have yet to notice or harness their own skills in this arena. People tend to trust those with psychic abilities, even if they aren't sure why they trust them. This can be for multiple reasons, from guidance, to support, to solving mysteries, or even a simple intuitive pull. When you learn to embrace these skills as blessings from nature, you can begin to put them toward helping the world.

Chapter 3:
Psychic Abilities 101

As we mentioned earlier, psychic abilities are there for anyone who wishes to use them. There are different senses that are used to deliver the psychic messages we pick up. These include:

- Touch (the knowledge that comes along with it, also called clairsentience)

- Hearing (access to sound frequencies that others cannot hear, also called clairaudience)

- Enhancement of sight (clairvoyance).

When we develop these senses, our connection with the spiritual energy of the universe grows, and we become wiser. People experience this energy and power every day, but simply aren't aware of what it is. You might think of it as simple intuition, sudden insight, or a strong feeling in your gut. To put it another way, this is the energy of the universe that is always present and can be tapped into at will.

What do these Abilities do for you?

When you strengthen and work with your natural abilities, you are opening your heart, mind, and ability to see. Doing this connects you with your truest nature as a creative being, where you are in touch with your imagination and deep senses. Before describing some of the most common psychic abilities, let's go over some more benefits to having and discovering them:

- **Finding your Destiny:** Tapping into your psychic skills gets you more in touch with yourself, and lets you work in collaboration with the spirit of this universe, to follow and discover your personal path in life. We are all a part of this energy, but most of us live as though this isn't true, and it makes us less powerful than we really are, at our core.

- **Seeing Beyond what is in Front of you:** When you strengthen and enhance your natural senses, you are accessing a plane beyond this world, in the spiritual realm. This allows you to interpret and see the world from a perspective that has been broadened. You will no longer be limited to what you can only see right in front of you, but can gain insight from many sources.

- **Allowing Solutions to Find you:** Have you ever noticed that when you stop worrying about a problem, the solution has a tendency to suddenly appear? This can become a common occurrence for you when you tap into your natural psychic abilities. You will be opening up an entirely new world to yourself, tapping into the universe behind logic.

Common Psychic Skills:

These are some of the possible psychic abilities or powers to have. Some people have all of them, while some only have one or two. Some people will easily be able to develop many of these skills, while for others it will take a lot more time and effort to develop only a couple of them. Every person is different, and are blessed with varying levels of natural ability.

- **The Gift of Clairvoyance:** This is the skill of being able to see reality past the common senses, and to see very clearly. Some call this intuition or the sixth human sense, and it mostly comes in colors or images in the mind. A reader who is skilled in this area can often see colors of auras, and sense issues with auras. When you receive a reading from a clairvoyant person, you should expect a reading that gives you direction in your life, along with clarity on problems you've been having. This should also point you to chances to take more control over your existence and life.

- A clairvoyant person is there to help you with setting and defining personal goals, coming up with possible actions for making them happen, figuring out what it is in life that brings you happiness and joy, and methods for becoming more peaceful. They do this in a unique way, using their third eye to grasp these intuitions. This calls upon the third eye chakra, and allows the reader to see images. However, seeing these images is only part of the work, and the rest of the work lies in interpreting their significance and relaying that information to the seeker of the information.

- This ability mostly relies on the right half of the brain, which is responsible for intuition and creative processes, rather than logic or analytic reasoning. This gift can be used to help people see what situations in their lives are causing problems, and what may happen if those problems aren't resolved. They can help you figure out which actions would be best and healthiest for you to take in any given situation, whether that be a relationship, family matter, or career choice.

- **The Skill of Clairaudience:** Also known as the ability to "hear beyond", this skill gives you the ability to get messages from the unseen universe, or world of spirit, through sounds. Many people use this skill without even knowing that they are doing it, when they listen to that small voice inside. These messages may come to you from a relative who has passed on, a spirit guide, or even nonphysical entities. These messages will typically aid you in your growth on a spiritual level, and help you see the patterns of your current path.

- These readings are useful for communicating with the dead, your highest version of self, or angels. Clairaudient readings are helpful for bringing closure both to a loved one that has passed away, and the relative left behind, and may even allow the two to communicate with each other. It's also possible to ask for answers to questions you have, by accessing this realm and using clairaudience. With the information that comes to you from that, you can become aligned in your physical, emotional, and mental life.

- Keep in mind that, although many authentic clairaudient readers exist, there are also scammers out there who just want your money. When you receive insights or messages from the realm beyond, do your best to verify the information you receive somehow before believing it right away.

- **The Ability of Clairsentience:** This skill relies on the ability to touch something and know about it, or to feel sensations in a heightened way. This is commonly known as a psychic power, since your senses of emotion, taste, touch, and even smell can all go into a state that is heightened and stronger than usual. For some, the feeling or emotional part will be overwhelming or extremely clear. This ability is a useful tool that anyone can access quite simply, just by paying close attention.

- Examples of this skill include the feelings you have in your gut, which steer you away from seemingly harmless events or people, which you later find out were trouble or would have been horrible. You might also have a feeling you should go somewhere you don't usually go, and find that something wonderful results from following that small feeling. Getting a reading from a clairsentient person can allow you to gain data from various sources of use to you.

- You may also come to possess knowledge about issues or people present in your current reality, which is often not what it seems. A crucial element of getting to know yourself and your feelings is making decisions that are informed, from a place of wisdom, so that you feel at ease when you act, instead of doubtful.

What do these Abilities Rely on?

It's clear that not everyone is in touch with these skills, but why is that? What is it that allows some to access these powers, and others to not even know they exist? Everyone who experiences these amazing abilities, harnesses their power, and benefits from them in daily life follows the following principles:

- **Acknowledging the Truth:** You cannot develop your abilities (which everyone has, as mentioned earlier) without first acknowledging that they are real and available to you. Should you simply accept this truth blindly? Of course not. Instead, research this subject thoroughly, reading any information on the subject that you can access, including articles and biographies. Look for patterns, or experiences that you recognize. When you actually look, you will start noticing psychic phenomena for what they are, instead of writing them off as simple coincidence.

- **Practicing your Skills:** All valuable skills require practice, and this subject is no different. You need to commit to practicing this each and every day, in a quiet and undisturbed place. Some find that calming music helps them get into the right frame of mind for this practice. You can then focus in on a peaceful and silent picture or scene of nature mentally. This will be your safe and quiet space that you should access each day. Once you make it to that spot, let your thoughts flow naturally, without forcing them. At the end of this practice, write your thoughts down.

- **Concentrating Fully:** When seemingly random ideas pop into your head, don't just ignore them or let them pass you by. Instead, focus in on them. These thoughts and ideas are coming up inside of you not randomly, but for good reason. You don't need to know or even wonder about why that is just yet. Focus first on just noticing what it is that's coming to you, and this should start making sense when you take action based on that information.

As you should know by now, psychic gifts are our right as humans, and are given to us as we enter this earth. Using these skills is less about gaining something new, and more about clearing out everything that is standing in the way. Fear is usually at the center of our resistance to anything new, including developing our psychic abilities.

<u>Facing your Fear to Tap into these Abilities:</u>

Fear holds us back in life, especially from our innate psychic abilities. We all know what it's like to fear failure in our life's pursuits. Getting in touch with your special abilities can help assuage this anxiety. When you operate from a place of fear, you can't think clearly or logically, and it gets harder and harder to solve your issues. You might even feel stagnate or stuck in repetitive actions that lead you nowhere. Our next chapter will give you steps on accessing your psychic skills, but you should first address the following issues:

- **Recognizing Fear:** In order to reach success and achieve our dreams, we have to know what it is we're afraid of, which will allow us to move on. Getting over your anxieties starts by recognizing them for what they are. Think this over carefully, writing down your thoughts in order to gain more clarity. What are your deepest fears? These can be related to your business, personal life, or personal relationships, which can play a role in your resistance to acknowledging your psychic powers.

- **Noticing Repetitive Thoughts:** Which thoughts are constantly repeating in your head, and what can they tell you about your deepest fears? Which area of your current experience is being held back by fear? Can you release these thoughts by noticing what they are?

Which seems more intimidating to you, ignoring your fear or facing it? You must first make sure that you're ready to face your anxieties before you do, if you wish to have success with this venture.

- **Know that these Fears have a Purpose:** Fear has a purpose, even if it can be a negative force, at times. It allows us to know that something is amiss, and that the way we are acting or thinking isn't aligned with our truer selves. Getting familiar with this idea can remove some of the negative association we have with the concept of fear, and help us see that it does, in fact, have its place in our life. Why are you afraid to recognize your own psychic abilities, and how can you move past this fear?

- **Where did they Come from?** Everything you are, right in this moment, is the result of what you were in the past. Pay attention to your specific fears, and find out where they came from. It could have come from someone specific, or one memory or experience. When those fears come back up, as they usually do, you only need to remind yourself that they aren't relevant to you anymore. Doing this allows you to create an empowered and positive stance that you don't need to own those thoughts, and can move on now into your true self and abilities.

It's a shame to go through your entire life without owning what is yours and using your abilities in the psychic realm. You need to first move past your fear in relation to this activity, using your frustration as fuel to achieve your goals. This will be your first conscious use of your psychic abilities. Once you have mastered this, you're ready to move onto the next chapter, which will tell you all about developing your psychic skills.

Chapter 4: Methods for Psychic Development

This chapter is here to give you ideas, techniques, and methods that will allow your innate gifts to blossom and shine. In order for this to be as effective as possible, you should do only one of these techniques per day, at first. There is no special order that they must be done in, and you can begin with whichever seems easiest or most appealing to you. In just a couple of months, you will be shocked at how much you've grown in this area.

<u>Psychic Development Practices to Start with:</u>

These are simply meant to point you in the right direction. Please feel free to combine any of the following exercises, or even to invent your own. This is meant to be inspiring and fun, so add your own personal twist to it for optimal results.

- **Scanning Energy:** This technique can be practiced with a relative or friend. Stand about five feet from them, both closing your eyes. Breathe deeply for a few minutes to get grounded, and then attempt to visualize them as a beam of energy, rather than solid or material. Pay attention to any symbols, numbers, words, or thoughts that come into your mind, including patterns or colors. Once a couple of minutes has passed, and you regain consciousness, tell your partner your thoughts and ideas, and listen to theirs.

- **Using your Skills of Prediction:** This art is one method for gauging how far you've come with your psychic skills. You can begin this in a simple way, next time your cellphone rings, pause and focus your attention on the call, and who you believe is trying to reach you. Another method you can use is trying to take the temperature of a room, sensing any emotions that are within it. This could be happiness, tenseness, or excitement. Focus in on the people in the room and try to see what they are feeling.

- Once you get into a habit of doing this, it will come automatically and your thoughts will come easily to you. You can confirm whether your feelings are correct or not by what transpires later on in that room. When you predicted that the temperature of the room was tense, did an argument break out? When you sensed happiness in the room, was the conversation positive and joyful?

- **Object Sensing:** Begin with items or objects that familiar people own. This is the best way to begin because once you have a feeling or thought toward the object, you can confirm whether or not it was correct. You can do this by holding an item and paying attention to any ideas or visions that appear in your mind, including scents or feelings. Since every item holds vibrations of history inside of it, these can be seen by you. Take some time to reflect on what you have picked up before sharing it with someone else. When you're ready, they can either confirm or deny your feelings.

- **Premonitions:** Every person out there has ideas of what will come, premonitions, or visions, that haven't occurred yet. This is because our minds are constantly sensing what is in this world and universe, although we may not realize that that is what's happening. Writing down these feelings can help you notice when your visions are correct. You can then notice when they happen or when they don't. When you start to pay attention to them, you can verify their reality or truth, but if you never pay attention, you will miss them altogether.

- **Noticing Impressions in the Mind:** Each morning, before getting caught up in your daily routine, pause to have some quiet time, and then ask the question "What will happen today?" Include details about how you will feel, who you will see, and any other details that come to you. Don't write off any impressions, because you can't know what is correct before giving it a chance. Once your day has ended, go over this list to see what you were correct about.

- **Meditation:** This should be done each and every day, for a minimum of 10 minutes each session. When you wish to develop your skills in the psychic realm, you have to raise your energy and vibration, since the energy of spirit is always at a frequency that is higher. To access this, and thus gain psychic benefits from it, meditation can be used. This state allows you to raise your vibration at will, as you enter a relaxed state of being. You will then be more connected to energy, yours, that of others, and that of the divine spirit.

- **Getting in Touch with Spirit Guides:** When you mediate, you can take this opportunity to meet your guides. As soon as you enter the relaxed state completely, request for your spirit guide or guides to make themselves known. Try to find out what their names are, and don't hold back on saying what you feel you should say. Have trust in the process, and allow your intuition to guide you.

- **Notice your Dreams:** In order to hone your psychic abilities, you should notice what your dreams are telling you. Notice the images coming through in your dreams, especially symbols that repeat themselves. There is a reason why these messages are coming through, so you should treat them with respect.

- **Practice Energy Readings on Objects:** This is a fun way to test your skills and practice your psychic abilities. You just need to place an object into your hands, or simply touch it. This should be something made of metal that has a lot of history or emotion attached to it, such as a sentimentally valuable piece of jewelry. Once you've done this, hold the object for a while and allow any information that may be there to come through to you, including names and emotions. Again this is best done with the object of someone you are familiar with, so you can confirm if your intuitions are correct.

- **Object Visualization:** You can improve your skills of clairvoyance using visualization. This is best done with natural objects, such as a stone or flower. Focus your attention completely on every detail of the object. This is meant to strengthen your powers of observation and get you in the habit of noticing detail, which will then translate over to your mental and psychic life.

- **General Visualization:** This is similar to the step above, but no specific object is necessary, and this can be entirely random. It's best to take on this step after you have already mastered the object visualization exercise. To do this method, get into a relaxed state, with your eyes closed, and place your attention on your brow, where your third eye is located. Ask for your guide to give you a peaceful and beautiful image to look at, and allow as many images to come through as you can. Try not to think too much, and instead allow your mind to rest without words.

- **Get Acquainted with Nature**: Taking a walk outside can help you get in touch with your latent psychic skills. You can even do a walking meditation out among the trees, focusing in on each step as you go, clearing your head and raising your energy levels. Since attaining psychic skills is more about clearing out the clutter that is standing in the way than anything else, this is a great way to do so.

- **Immerse yourself in Related Writing**: The best way to get in the flow of any new path is to read and think about it often. There are plenty of valuable resources out there on this subject, to be found on the internet or in your local library. Also the simple act of focusing on this subject will help you stay in the zone.

- **Go to Antique Shops**: Next time you visit a shop full of old stuff, pay attention to how you're feeling when you're there. Browse the store and pick up some items, noticing whether anything comes to you, such as a vision, a name, or anything else. This is great practice for a developing psychic, since these old objects will have existing memories and histories within each of them.

- **Keep a Psychic Development Journal**: This is an important step. Information from the realm beyond can come to you in many different ways, and oftentimes is meant to be metaphorical or symbolic. Since this information seems to appear to you at random, it can be hard to make sense of it all, which is where recording your findings down in a journal comes in. Your guide is there to help you both notice and interpret the data that comes through to you. Not only will this allow you to record your progress, but you can also review it in a few months to see how far you've come on your journey.

- It's easy to lose track of how much progress we're making until we see proof of where we once were, and journal entries can be great for this reason. At the end of the day, review each sentence you wrote to see if you notice any patterns emerging or other relevant information. Write everything down, however seemingly insignificant, because it may make sense later.

- Writing is a key way to stay in touch with your higher or divine self, which is responsible for your psychic gifts. Don't forgo this valuable chance to connect with that part of you.

- **Research related Material:** This can include chakras and auras. Seeing auras is another psychic skill that anyone can do. You can practice this on yourself or a friend. Make sure that there is a solid wall behind your friend or you, and try to focus on the space that surrounds the body. After a while, you should notice that the air is shimmering in this area. As you practice this skill more and more, you may start to notice colors.

- **Practice Hearing beyond**: Part of developing your psychic skills is paying attention to what you would have previously ignored or not seen as significant. When you are falling asleep at night, sit quietly and pay attention to every sound you can hear. Paying attention to these noises, which you might not regularly notice, will help you strengthen your gift of hearing, both of this world and beyond.

- **Give Readings**: If you wish to develop your psychic abilities or even become a medium, this is a key step. It's just like developing any other skill; the more you practice it, the better you get. Find some interested or willing friends and put your skills to the test. If it doesn't go the way you wished it would, at first, don't worry, it's normal to take a while to get good at this, and it will come with time and dedication.

- **Look at Old Pictures**: Look through some of your family's old pictures and see if you can notice anything about relatives you've never known. This can be a great way to test your instincts, because you can confirm your findings with a living relative who did know the deceased family member, to see if you were right.

- **Find Likeminded Friends:** It helps a lot to have friends with similar interests as you, when exploring a new skill. Join a circle or class about becoming psychic, which will allow you access to likeminded people. You can then practice your skills with them, and they can practice theirs with you. Getting to know other mediums or aspiring psychics is an interesting pursuit.

- **Practice Turning on and off your Abilities**: When you begin to follow this path, it's important to figure out how to control your skills. When your abilities are turned on constantly, you are in danger of absorbing energies that you shouldn't absorb. Doing a positivity meditation and then asking your guide to protect you should suffice for this. You also need to know how to shut the skills off when you need to. You can do this by thanking your guide for helping you, and saying goodbye.

The Importance of a High Vibration:

One of the most crucial elements of honing your psychic gifts is making sure you always have a high vibration. You cannot tap into your psychic gifts without making sure this base is covered first and foremost. This is needed because:

- You are matching the vibration of spirit.

- Living a high vibration existence means being authentic and joyful, making you more connected to yourself and able to tap into your skills.

- Staying in this vibration means attracting similar souls to you, who you can relate to and have great relationships with.

The Importance of Health and Positivity:

Although some may believe that health and attitude are independent from intuition or psychic abilities, they are all quite connected.

- **Positivity**: This state of being is a must for your psychic pursuits, because if you don't believe you can, you aren't likely to achieve your goals. When you are positive, you are less likely to doubt your feelings about things, and those are what make you psychic in the first place. If you are full of doubt about yourself, how are you to reach your fullest potential? Pay close attention to your attitude toward yourself on this journey.

- Practice positivity exercises such as affirmations, gratitude meditations, and focusing on love and light throughout the day. Tell yourself that you are a worthwhile and valuable person with many gifts to share with this world. This will help you to stay positive.

- **Physical Health**: Part of being in a state of high vibration is paying attention to your health, which relies heavily on positivity. When you eat healthier foods, such as vegetables and fruit, you are helping your body perform at its highest capacity. A healthy physical body leads to better mental and emotional energy, and a crystal clear mind is helpful in honing your psychic talents.

Don't forget that this journey is meant to be fun, and being in a high vibrational state relies a lot on that very quality. Follow what your heart tells you and remember to keep this light-hearted and joyful. Whenever it starts to stray from that, it's time to take a break and revisit it when you feel more positive. This will help protect you from negative entities and help you to stay on a good path.

Chapter 5:
How to do a Psychic Meditation Practice

Learning how to do a psychic mediation practice is helpful if you wish to develop your psychic skills and talents. When you commit yourself to this practice, and to doing it each and every day, you will likely discover what you are looking for within yourself. You can do this with an image that you enjoy, a mental picture, physical objects such as candles or crystals, or anything that you feel is relevant to aiding your abilities. The key here is doing it each day. It's less important which specific practice you choose for meditation, and more important that you are consistent and dedicated to it.

How Long should you Meditate for?

You should meditate once a day for at least 10 minutes at a time. Contrary to what some believe, this process is not complex or complicated at all. Just find somewhere where you won't be disturbed and pay attention to your breathing. Thoughts will pop up in your mind, which is to be expected and totally normal. Simply let them go after acknowledging their presence. Keep breathing very deeply, and allow yourself to feel this moment. This will connect you with your higher self and allow you to feel centered and grounded in this world.

What is Psychic Meditation all About?

This type of meditation might be different than you're used to, since you're seeking a specific outcome from this, instead of general relaxation or calm in your mind. If you don't know how to meditate, refer to the previous chapter for the simple breath meditation, which is a great starting point. Here are some key differences to take note of, that you can add to your breath meditation practice when you feel ready to do so:

- **Using Stones:** Some find it helpful to use a crystal, and clear quartz is recommended. These can be found on the internet or even in a specialty shop in your local area. You might also find a stone out in nature that you are drawn to for some reason, which could work for your meditation.

- **Calling upon your Guide(s):** Ask for your spirit guide or guides to join you and show you the way. You might notice certain feelings or visual depictions appearing in your mind during this step. Focus also and call upon your divine self.

- **Focus on your Brow, then Higher**: Now you should focus on a bright white light in your mind, and bring it up to your brow, or third eye area, which allows you to enter into a higher realm of spirit. Now, bring your attention even higher, to your crown area. Picture your consciousness rising up, as though you are on a spiritual elevator.

- **Picture Yourself**: Now you should try to see your own body below where your consciousness is floating, and envision that you are looking far down at it. Your brain may slow down here, and your eyelids might start fluttering. Let yourself release any anxiety or tension now, becoming completely relaxed. Tune into the silence all around you, and allow it to become a part of your body and entire being.

- **Stay Aware and Focused**: Now is the important part. Stay entirely aware and focused on what is happening. In this state of mind, it's much easier to sense messages coming to you, whether they are visual, auditory, or feeling-related. You have to simply recognize that these signals are there for you to see and notice. Make sure you are grateful for this and acknowledge that, as well. You may find it helpful to call again upon your guide or guides, if you haven't picked anything up yet at this point.

- **Stay there a While**: You have the freedom to remain in this state for as long or short as you wish, but a minimum of 10 minutes a day will get you the results you are seeking. You will be teaching your brain to reach this place when you need to contact your guides, and you can also reduce your stress significantly by following this practice. Keep in mind that your guides may wish to present themselves in any number of various ways. Stay calm and let them show up the way they wish to, and trust that it is all happening as it should.

- **Notice Colors that Appear to you**: Colors are closely related to the realm of spirits, and you might notice some when you do your psychic meditation practice. These could be an indication of a feeling state of your own which you must acknowledge, or perhaps that of someone close to you. It's up to your own interpretation and discernment to find this out, though you can call upon your guide or guides for help, if you wish to do so.

<u>What to Expect with Regular Practice:</u>

It's wonderful what you can be shown or told in this state that can help you on your path in life. You may even notice very overwhelming sensations of joy and peace. Doing this meditation every day will benefit you in a number of ways, including stress reduction and a heightened level of awareness. This process is not instant and doesn't happen immediately, although you might notice your skills developing very quickly. There is no specific level that you should be trying to reach here, since this is an ongoing journey and practice.

Chapter 6:
Signs your Abilities are Improving

When you start to follow this path of developing your psychic skills, you will probably want a way to measure if you're progressing. This chapter will cover signs that show you that your skills are coming to life and waking up. These skills can start appearing during any age in your life. Although everyone is born with these gifts, if you aren't surrounded by encouragement about using them, they get rusty and forgotten. However, these gifts can be awakened spontaneously throughout life, or with time and effort, which you may have noticed, or may be noticing now.

<u>Signs that your Psychic Gifts are Active:</u>

- **A New Social Circle:** Most individuals who pursue an awakening in their consciousness will notice that a new social circle appears as they begin growing their psychic gifts. You might find that your old friends don't interest you anymore, or that they have lost interest in you. This is okay, and entirely normal. Everyone outgrows friends as their interests shift, and when you are flourishing in this arena, you will likely see this earth in a new way, and start growing in a different direction than your old friends.

- You will feel curious and excited and wish to engage in meaningful, rich conversations and friendships. Although it's fun to talk about trivial things sometimes, it won't be enough to hold your interest anymore, for long. Instead, you'll be on the hunt for depth and meaning. This may be lonely for you, if you haven't met new friends that match your vibration yet, but don't worry, this will change in time.

- **Healthier Interests:** When your psychic gifts begin to awaken, you might notice that you start craving healthy activities, such as eating nutritional foods, walking out in nature more, exercising more, and cutting out negative activities like drinking or smoking. Following habits like this makes us feel better on a spiritual, emotional, and physical level, and this knowledge comes to you intuitively. In addition to this, you are no longer interested in masking your feelings with distractions, such as unhealthy activities on a regular basis.

- **You are Full of Insights:** When your gifts start to come to life, you will be full of insights, and although you might have noticed your intuition before in life, it will now be kicked into overdrive. You may even have a sense that a spirit is guiding you, and be on the receiving end of signals that are not ignorable. If this is completely new to your way of thinking, it's worth taking some time to figure out how your feelings and intuition function. It's different for everyone, and this can help you understand this journey in a bigger picture sense.

- **An Active Third Eye:** Once your abilities begin to show up, your brow chakra (also known as your third eye) might start to feel different, or even tingle. This happens to many people, and comes along with strengthening clairvoyant abilities. You may also notice an increase in visions along with this new change.

- **Heightened Physical Sensitivity:** When your psychic senses start to grow, your ordinary senses might also become more sensitive. This includes your sense of touch, sight, hearing, and more. For you, there may be a particular sense that seems to be heightened. Pay close attention to this, because it could be your gift or specialty in the psychic realm.

- **You Sense Presences Around You:** When you awaken these abilities within yourself, you may feel spirits around you. Not all psychics become mediums, but some do, and this could be a sign that this is an option for you. You might be picking up messages from your deceased loved ones, or even those of your friends. Pay close attention to what you see and feel in regards to this, it could be significant.

- **Your Dreams Change:** In the waking world, our perception guards us against input that we do not recognize. Many people have feelings of an extrasensory nature, but simply ignore them out of habit, writing it off as coincidence or imagination. When you're sleeping, however, your logical brain also rests and your higher self can show you important messages. When your dreams become extra vivid or symbolic, this is a sign that your gifts are awakening within you.

- **You Feel Energies Easily:** Once your abilities begin to truly flow, you become sensitive to all energies. You might feel repelled by certain events, people, or places, for no apparent reason that you can explain. You might find that reading or watching the news is no longer tolerable, because you can sense the pain of others in such a clear way. You might be very repelled by drama in your social circle and find it exhausting, draining, and not worth any thought.

- **You Get Headaches More Often:** Along with the awakening of your skills in this area, you may notice that you feel headaches more often than before. This is because you are accessing a part of yourself that has possibly been dormant for quite some time. You will get used to this, however, and the aches will fade. Eventually, you will be centered and grounded in the present moment, with your abilities. If this starts happening very often to you, it's time to take a break and rest.

If you recognized any of these signs, especially more than one, your abilities are likely waking up. Hopefully this has given you some peace of mind. Similar to any other new interest, it may be unfamiliar and uncomfortable when you first begin, but it's all part of the growth process. Don't feel bad about being different than others; this will help you progress a lot in life. When you feel drawn to the psychic realm, intuition, and all that is spiritual, that is your destiny and path to follow. This should be celebrated!

Chapter 7:
The Different Psychic Abilities

Every single person possesses some level of psychic ability naturally, and their skills can always be further developed. However, there are many different ways that psychic abilities can present themselves. Some people will be naturally gifted in certain areas, and not so much in others. It is a great idea to discover what natural talents you have, and then work on improving these skills further.

Below is a detailed list of the most common psychic abilities that exist. Take note if you have experienced any of these things for yourself, and those will be great skills to continue to practice and develop further!

Clairvoyance

A clairvoyant is a person who can clearly see non-physical realities and entities. These people can often view auras, energies, spirits, and different entities.

Clairaudience

Clairaudience is the ability to hear events occurring in another place, or even in another dimension. It is similar to clairvoyance, but instead of actually seeing the energies, spirits, activities, and entities – clairaudients hear them.

Clairsensitivity

A person who is clairsensitive can feel surrounding energies, spirits, and activities. This may come as a physical sensation, or as an overwhelm of a particular emotion. Many clairsensitive people also get these messages through the sense of smell.

Remote-Viewing

Remote viewing is also sometimes referred to as travelling clairvoyance. A remote viewer can see things happening in another location, be it physical or not. Often this occurs in real-time, with their eyes open.

Astral Travel

Astral travel is the ability to travel along the astral plane, to another location. This occurs during sleep. Normally, this involves the astral traveler visualizing themselves leaving their physical body, attached by a long cord. From here, astral travelers are free to roam wherever they wish, communicate with other entities, and visit other places – be them physically real or not. People have been said to astral travel to locations, and gleam information that proved to be 100% correct in reality. Some astral travelers also use their skills to communicate with other people and entities during their travels.

Lucid Dreamer

A lucid dreamer is somebody who can control their dreams. A lot of people naturally have this ability when they are young, but lose it over time. It can however, be developed and worked upon. This is related to astral projection, and many people learn to become lucid dreamers before stepping into the world of astral travel.

Pre-cognition

Pre-cognition is the ability to gather information from the future. This information is not always correct, as future events can be changed based on the pre-cognitor's actions.

Retro-Cognition

Retro-cognition is the ability to gather information from the past. This can also mean information gathered from the past in a non-physical dimension. This can come in the form of visions of the past, certain emotions, voices, smells and a general sense of an event occurring.

Telepathy

Telepathy is the ability to communicate from mind-to-mind. It is the ability to send messages, simply via thought to another human. Some advanced telepaths are able to send and receive very clear messages to one another. Most people have experienced some level of telepathy before. A common occurrence is thinking strong thoughts about another person, and then all of a sudden, that person rings them.

Psychography

A psychographer is a person who does automatic writing, or psychic writing. Another energy or entity takes control of what the person writes, and they often subconsciously are able to communicate messages through writing or drawing. The psycographer simply dictates, either consciously or subconsciously.

Medium

A medium is a person who brings information from the non-physical dimension, to the physical dimension. They 'mediate' the information. Everyone has a certain level of medium ability. Mediums can work in a variety of ways, from telepathy, to psychography, to having visions that they relay.

Psychophoning

Psychophoning is when a non-physical consciousness or entity uses your physical body to speak. This can happen both consciously and subconsciously. This can be a frightening phenomenon for many, as the medium may not be in control of the experience.

Psychic Healing

Psychic healing is the ability to use energy to heal yourself or another person. The psychic healer uses intense focus to direct healing energy to the person with an ailment, either in person or from a distance. It requires intense visualization and focus to achieve, but has existed in many forms throughout history – such as Reiki healing.

Aural Viewing

Aural viewing is the ability to view another person's aura. An aura is an energy field of colors that surround a person's body. It can be viewed both in person and also through photographs. The different colors of an aura indicate a person's emotions and energy that they are emitting. It can point to different health problems, and also provide an indication of a person's true character.

Telekinesis

Telekinesis is the ability to move objects with your mind. You may have seen people who can bend spoons with their mind – that is an example of this ability!

Chapter 8:
Spirit Guides

Many different cultures and belief systems make reference to the existence of spirit guides. According to the belief system, sometimes they appear as animals, people, energies, or even deceased relatives or friends.

Spirit guides exist to help you to achieve your purpose on this earth, and to provide protection for you. As their name suggests, they are here simply to guide you on your journey in the physical realm.

Who Are Your Spirit Guides?

So, who are your spirit guides? For every person, it is different and often personal. You may have just one spirit guide, or multiple, and some may only exist through certain periods of your life.

These guides will exist at different levels also. Some will be lower level beings such as an animal, or can be of a higher level such as a religious figure. These guides have different purposes and will be with you for varying periods of time. They are all there to simply help you through certain periods of struggle, triumph, goals, and obstacles. Each has their own unique set of skills and purpose in your life.

Your guides may be only assisting you, or perhaps other people also. Spirit guides are essentially energy. Some people can communicate with spirit guides, whilst others never know of their existence. In some cases, your spirit guide may be a deceased relative or pet, though this is not too common.

What Do These Guides Do?

It is the duty of your spirit guides to steer you through life. They are not there to make decisions for you, but they can help encourage you to make the correct choices. During periods of time where their intervention is needed, they will often make contact through the form of a subtle sign that many people fail to realize, or even ignore.

How Do Spirit Guides Send Signs?

There are a range of different ways that your spirit guide might send a signal to you. This might be in the form of something you continually see. Perhaps you see the same word everywhere, or the same number. This might have a particular meaning to you at that point in time.

Spirit guides can also cause you to have 'gut feelings'. Have you ever just had a feeling in your gut that something was about to go wrong, and then it did. Or you had a gut feeling about turning down a certain street, or approaching a certain person, and the results were life-changing? Those are examples of a gut feeling, and can often be attributed to your spirit guides.

They can be responsible for the intuitive voice in your head that says 'slow down', right before an accident occurs. These guides will send people into your life at influential moments, and help guide you to places you need to be.

Your spirit guides are constantly keeping an eye on you, and sending signals to help you safely continue along your intended path.

How To Communicate With Your Guides

So, how can you directly contact your guides for further insight and discussion? Below are a few different methods for beginning to better communicate with your guides.

- The first step is to begin listening to your intuition. Start listening to that voice in your head that says 'go and talk to her' or 'don't go down that street'. Those intuitive feelings are often the work of a spirit guide, and beginning to focus on them will open up for more and more communication between you and your guide.

- Next, you need to start looking for signs, and taking note of them. Is your guide sending you subtle messages that maybe you're not taking note of? Are you constantly running into the same person, seeing the same video everywhere, seeing a number or word all around you? These are examples of signs. Take note of them, and consider different ways that they might be related to your current situation.

- Another great thing to do is journal. Every night, journal about the different things that happened during the day, and signs that appeared. This will help you to better understand patterns, recognize signs that you may not have noticed before, and understand what your guide is trying to tell you. You might not notice a sign right away, but looking back on your journal entries after things have unfolded can make those signs seem pretty obvious in hindsight!

- Meditation is a fantastic way to begin communicating with your guide. Some people who reach deep meditative states can physically see or feel their guides during these states. When you meditate, ask for your guides to appear before you, or communicate with you in some way. The more you do this, the stronger the bond with your guide will become, and the easier it will be to communicate with them.

- Dreaming is another way in which you can communicate with your guides. Many people have psychic experiences during their sleep, mostly comprising of visions. Sleep is similar to a meditative state, where you are more open to communication with different energies. For those that lucid dream regularly, this will be a lot easier. Before sleep, focus a lot on communicating with your guides, and verbally invite them to communicate with you through your dreams.

Spirit guides are positive beings that are there to help you throughout your journey on this planet. When communicating with your guides, you should only feel a positive energy. If a negative or evil vibe is present, they are likely not your guides and you should cease communication with them at once.

Opening up communication with your spirit guides is a great thing to do, and will assist you in staying out of danger, getting through tough periods of your life, and achieving the things that you strive for!

Chapter 9:
Third Eye Awakening

Many different cultures make reference to a third eye, situated between the brows. In these cultures, this third eye is heavily connected with psychic abilities. This third eye is said to exist in all of us, though many of us need to 'awaken' the eye to really unlock our psychic prowess.

Due to a number of factors, the third eye usually lies dormant. People often neglect their intuition and psychic abilities that they are born with, which causes the third eye to 'lock up' in a sense.

If you can manage to unlock its power, your psychic abilities will greatly improve and be readily available to you.

The Third Eye In Different Cultures

The third eye is mentioned in many different cultures, religions, and belief systems. Each particular group has their own beliefs surrounding it, but all make reference to its incredible power and connection with higher abilities.

It is mentioned in Hinduism as the 'anja' or 'brow chakra'. In Hindiusm it is believed to be the 6th chakra, and can be trained to become stronger, much like a muscle can be.

Taoism and many other Chinese religions also make reference to a third eye. They believe that by focusing on the third eye and its vibrations, a very deep level of meditation may be reached.

Some theosophists believe that the third eye is in fact a dormant pineal gland. Some believe that through training, the third eye can be developed to allow for higher abilities.

The Third Eye Chakra

As previously mentioned, in Hinduism the third eye is believed to be the 6th chakra, also know as 'anja' or the 'brow chakra'.

In order to make proper use of your third eye, the preceding chakras must be clear and unblocked. The energy flow begins at the 1st chakra and flows upward toward the brown chakra where the third eye exists. Many believe that unblocking and balancing the chakras is the key to making full use of the third eye, and getting the most out of your psychic abilities.

The Pineal Gland

As previously mentioned, some theosophists believe that the third eye in in fact a dormant, or calcified, Pineal gland. The Pineal gland is a gland in the brain, in the same position that the third eye is said to exist.

It has no known function, and so many believe that it is a gland that over time has become primarily dormant in humans. People believe that the third eye can be trained like a muscle to improve its function. This training is believed by some to improve the function of the Pineal Gland, allowing for better use of the third eye!

So, How Do You Awaken The Third Eye?

As you now know, the third eye lays dormant in most people. Nobody knows what causes this for sure. It could be a chakra blockage, a dormant pineal gland, or a lack of mindfulness. It all depends on which particular group you ask. The thing they all agree on though is that the third eye can be trained and awakened.

So how do we do this?

Firstly, it's important to understand that this is not a rapid process by any means. It will be faster for some, but usually it will take a continued effort and the use of many different strategies.

Once factor that appears to have a large effect on the third eye is your diet. In order to awaken your third eye, it is recommended that you avoid consuming any fluoride, eat a range of healthy organic fruits and vegetables, and avoid processed foods with chemical additives.

Another technique that is commonly used to awaken the third eye is sun gazing. This involves gazing at the sun during sunrise and sunset, and is believed to help de-calcify the pineal gland.

Meditation is another common method, used by many different groups. It is said to help activate and heal your chakras, and allow for energy to easily flow up through to the third eye. Focus on the third eye area whilst meditation. Some people will experience a pressure, or vibrating feeling between the brows when meditating. That's a clear sign that you're activating and strengthening your third eye.

Chanting is often combined with meditation when helping to awaken the third eye. Chanting 'om' is said to cause the tetrahedron bone in your nose to vibrate, stimulating the area where the third eye is situated.

Crystals are another method that you can implement. Crystals have been used by many different cultures for healing different ailments. When trying to improve the health of your third eye and awaken it, you can use amethyst, laser quartz, moonstone, pietersite, purple sapphire, purple violet tourmaline, rhodonite, rose aura, and sodalite. You can carry these with you, or place them between your brows whilst meditating.

All of these different method will help to awaken your third eye. The required method will be different for everyone, and the timeframe to awaken your third eye will vary also. It is best to use a combination of the above methods regularly, and you should notice your third eye awakening slowly, and your psychic abilities improving!

Chapter 10:
Chakras

Chakras are the different points in your body, through which energy flows. They were first mentioned somewhere from 1500 to 500 BC in the Vedas, the oldest known text.

There are 7 different chakras, and as briefly mentioned in the previous chapter, they are connected with your third eye and subsequently, your psychic abilities. If one of your chakras is blocked or unbalanced, the energy will not be able to flow onto the next one.

The energy flow starts at the bottom, in your sacral chakra, and works its way up through each energy point until it hits the top of your head, the crown chakra. The crown chakra is said to be where true enlightenment is achieved, and very few manage to have all of their preceding chakras working well enough to use it to its full potential.

In this chapter, we will discuss the 7 different chakras, what areas they relate to, and how to unblock and balance them in order to further enhance your psychic skills.

The 7 Chakras

Chakra 1 – Root Chakra

The Root Chakra represents our foundation. It provides us with a feeling of being grounded.

It is located at the very base of your spine, in the tailbone region.

It has emotional connections with issues such as: survival, financial stability, and the ability to access food. This Chakra in a way represents and is a reflection of our basic needs for survival.

When this Chakra is blocked or out of balance, greediness will be present. When it is clear and healthy, feelings of security, and a connection to the earth will be felt.

Chakra 2 – Sacral Chakra

The Sacral Chakra represents out connection to others and our ability to accept other people. It also represents our ability to accept new experiences.

It is located in the lower abdomen region, about 2 inches below the naval, and 2 inches in.

It has emotional connections with issues such as: a sense of abundance, our well-being, pleasure, and sexuality.

When this Chakra is blocked or out of balance, jealousy, anger, and codependency can be present. When it is clear and healthy, feelings of creativity and love will be felt.

Chakra 3 – Solar Plexus Chakra

The Solar Plexus Chakra represents our ability to be confident, and in control of ourselves and our lives.

It is located in the upper-abdomen, in the stomach region.

It has emotional connections with issues such as: self-worth, self-confidence, and self-esteem.

When this Chakra is blocked or out of balance, fear, guilt, and intimidation will be present. When it is clear and healthy, feelings of trust, self-esteem, confidence, and responsibility may be felt.

Chakra 4 – Heart Chakra

The Heart Chakra represents our ability to love.

It is located in the center of the chest, just above the heart.

It has emotional connections with issues such as: love, our ability to be loved and receive love, happiness, and inner peace.

When this Chakra is blocked or out of balance, resentment, hate, and loneliness may be present. When it is clear and healthy, feelings of peace, love, and connection to other/the environment may be felt.

Chakra 5 – Throat Chakra

The Throat Chakra represents our ability to communicate.

It is located in the middle of the throat.

It has emotional connections with issues such as: communication, our ability to express ourselves, our feelings, and the truth.

When this Chakra is blocked or out of balance, resentment, criticism, and addiction may be present. When it is clear and healthy, feelings of being balanced, the ability to easily express oneself, and the power of choice may be felt.

Chakra 6 – Third Eye Chakra (Also called the 'Brow Chakra')

The Third Eye Chakra represents our ability to see the big picture.

It is located between the eyes.

It has emotional connections with issues such as: imagination, intuition, wisdom, knowledge, and the ability to be decisive and have constructive thoughts.

When this Chakra is blocked or out of balance, learning difficulties or a tendency to lie may be present. When it is clear and healthy, feelings of great intuition may exist.

Chakra 7 – Crown Chakra

The Crown Chakra represents our ability to be fully connected spiritually.

It is located at the very top of the head.

It has emotional connections with issues such as: our beauty both inside and out, our connection to spirituality, and pure peace.

When this Chakra is blocked or out of balance, genetic disorders and selfishness may be present. When it is clear and healthy, feelings of being spiritually connected, and being at peace with God and the world may be felt.

How to Unblock & Heal Your Chakras

In order to activate the Third Eye and unlock your psychic potential, we must first unblock and heal any issues in the Chakras below it.

You first need to analyze the list of the Chakras, and see if you have any symptoms of that Chakra being blocked. Start with the first Chakra and then work your way upwards.

Be honest with yourself about what issues may be present that are causing that particular blockage.

The best way to unblock and heal your Chakras begins with introspection. You must first be honest with yourself and identify that you have an emotional issue/s related to one (or more) of the Chakras. You then must delve deeper into the issue, and really understand why that it is occurring.

This can be quite a painful experience and it can bring up bad memories, but it is a necessary part of the process. You must be able to understand the emotional issues that at present (and we all have them), be able to accept them for what they are, and make a conscious effort to move on from them in a positive direction.

Chakra blockages can be for a short period of time, or for an extended period. They are commonly caused by emotional issues, but can also be caused by personality traits, and physical ailments/intoxication. Further, they can be blocked by a simple lack of use.

Identifying any emotional issues or personality traits that may be negatively affecting the Chakras, and making an effort to move on from them, is a great first step. However, this is often not enough. Most people have forgotten their ability to control the energy in their body, and this must be re-learned.

The greatest way to do this is through focus and meditation.

A common method is to do what is known as 'energy breathing'. In this exercise you focus on your breath in a meditative state, and visualize the breath as glowing energy. You need to imagine this energy entering your body, and moving through each of the Chakras, starting at the bottom and rising up to the top. Feel and focus on the sensation of the energy as it touches and activates each of your Chakras, flowing smoothly on to the next. Feel yourself let go of any emotional issues that relate to the particular Chakra as your direct your energy to it.

Many people prefer to perform this exercise outdoors in nature, as it provides a greater connection to the earth and gets you away from any external distractions.

Different people use a multitude of modalities to unlock, unblock, and heal the different Chakras. Some people use meditation, some people use therapy and introspection, some use chanting, and some use crystals. All methods have their merits, but the best course of action is to begin by identifying the blockage in the first place, and why it has occurred. Overcoming the issues surrounding the occurrence of said blockage will help tremendously in healing your Chakras, and as a result, in your overall emotional wellbeing also.

Chapter 11:
Auras

Aural viewing is a common psychic ability that many people can develop. An aura is essentially an energy field that surrounds a person. This energy field will appear as a glow, and will often consist of many different colors.

To the untrained eye, an aura is invisible. However, auras can become visible to many people through training. They can be viewed in person, and also often times in photographs also.

The different colors that appear in a person's aura will tell the viewer things about their health, both mental and physical, the person's personality, and also their intentions. A person's aura is a reflection of them, and will reveal everything, both the good and the bad.

How to View Auras

So, how do you go about viewing a person's aura? This involves several steps, and often a good amount of practice. As you practice and improve your psychic abilities, this will become easier and easier.

There are several different methods used for aural viewing, but the easiest is to begin with a person standing still in front of a white wall. You can also use objects that are not alive, as these often have auras also.

It is important that the room is lit softly. You don't want it to be dim, nor do you want an overly bright room.

Stand back several feet from your subject at a distance that feels comfortable to you.

You then need to close your eyes, take several deep breaths, and relax. You need to be in a calm state for this to work. When you are calm, open your eyes and look at your subject. Don't focus on any one point, but rather allow your gaze to focus on nothing. Let them relax, while staring in the direction of your subject.

Your focus should be gentle, like when you are daydreaming. Soon, you should begin to see a milky color sort of floating around your subject. Keep looking steadily and the aura should become more clear. Colors will slowly come into focus and the aura will become easier and easier to see.

This process can take a lot of regular practice to develop and to become quicker at. After a while however, you may be able to quickly notice the auras of people and objects around you.

What the Different Colors Mean

A person's aura can tell you a lot about them, but how do you decipher what the aura is telling you?

The different colors provide big clues as to what's going on with the person! It's very rare for a person to just have one aura color, and normally it will be a mixture of different colors. Here are what the different colors mean:

- Rainbow Auras: These auras are found in healers, and those trained to work with the body's energy fields. They typically appear as shards of different colors.

- Yellow: A yellow aura is related to a person's spleen and also their energy source, often referred to as 'chi'. A bright yellow represents spiritual awakening and a playful spirit. A dark yellow with brown parts represents someone who is usually a student, and is feeling pressure to achieve things. Lemon yellow represents a fear of loss, and a pale yellow represents that someone has embarked on a spiritual journey.

- Orange: Orange is associated with the reproductive organs. A bright orange represents good health and vibrancy. An orange with red parts indicates confidence and a feeling of personal power. Finally, an orange with yellow parts represents a scientific mind, and perfectionist tendencies.

- Red: Red is one of the most powerful colors, and can be both good and bad. It represents the blood. A dark red suggests that a person is grounded to the earth and are self-sufficient. A brilliant red represents passion, and a competitive spirit. Clouded red represents anger.

- Pink: Generally, this color represents that a person is loving, and is also commonly seen in artists. If you've fallen in love, you will probably have a large amount of pink in your aura. On the contrary, dark pink represents deceit, dishonesty, and immaturity.

- Blue: Blue represents the throat, particularly the thyroid. If your aura is blue, you love helping people and have the ability to remain calm during times of great stress. Royal blue represents that you are highly developed spiritually and are clairvoyant. This color may become more evident as your skills further develop. A dark, cloudy blue represents a fear of the truth and the things the future may hold. A light blue however, represents a sense of truthfulness and sincerity, and excellent communication skills.

- Green: Green is the color of nature, and is very commonly seen in the auras of healers, teachers, and people who work to help the greater good. A forest green represents someone who is a born healer. A green with yellow bits represents someone who is a good communicator, normally an actor, writer, performer, or salesperson. A dark, cloudy green represents jealousy and resentment. And finally, a turquoise color is the ultimate color for a powerful healer! It is commonly seen in doctors and counselors.

- Purple: This color is associated with the pituitary gland, pineal gland, and the nervous system. A violet color represents those who are extremely visionary. This can be seen in people who change the world through loving actions. An indigo color represents someone with high psychic abilities, that can often get glimpses into other worlds.

- Silver: This color represents abundance. If it shines bright, it suggests a great level of physical and spiritual health.

- Gold: Gold represents protection. If this color is present, it means that the person has divine entities, such as spirit guides, present and protecting them.

- Black: Black auras represent negativity. They usually mean an unwilling and unforgiving spirit. This color can also represent disease. Depending on where it is located on a person's body, it can point to an illness in that particular area.

- White: This color indicates purity. It can be seen in spiritual people who have transcended. According to some religions, white auras surround angelic beings.

The colors of a person's aura can mean many different things, and will often change as their emotions change, and their journey in life progresses.

When reading auras, it is important to take note of all of the different colors present. Pay particular attention to the head area, as often this has the most meaning. Auras in this area will appear as somewhat of a glowing halo, and can provide great insight into the person.

Conclusion

Thanks again for taking the time to read this book!

You should now have a good understanding of the different psychic abilities, and know the necessary steps to develop your own skills further! I wish you the best of luck in your journey!

If you enjoyed this book, please take the time to leave me a review on Amazon. I appreciate your honest feedback, and it really helps me to continue producing high quality books.